Concentration is the ability to control your thoughts and organize your knowledge into a plan of action that is sound and workable.
Nothing was ever created by a human which was not first created in the imagination, through desire, then transformed into reality through concentration.

**Napoleon Hill, The Law of Success**

Concentration is one of the key currencies of today's world. That's where the most value is: in your ability to concentrate on your chief aim, one task at a time.

**Joseph Rodrigues, YouTube Creator**

# PRAISE FOR G.R.O.W.

This book is an absolute gift to the world. It's affirming, practical, grounding, and a timely resource for us all!
**Mariel Buqué, Ph.D.**
**Psychologist & Generational Trauma Expert**

As a creative, a perfectionist, and a perpetual over thinker, I am so grateful to have these tools that help me to engage my dream projects with love, ease, and affirmation! This productivity guide is perfect for folks like me who get overwhelmed easily, who sometimes feel like our goals are too big to achieve, who just need a little hand holding as we prepare action plans towards achieving our wildest dreams.
**dr. reelaviolette botts-ward,**
**Author of mourning my inner[blackgirl]child**

As an artist & innovator from Baltimore. I always had big ideas and dreams, some of which didn't even feel possible to achieve. Especially having self doubts that would affect my confidence, & self-expression.

This productivity guide is allowing me to take my goals one step at a time, while I'm discovering new things about myself and creativity, which takes the mountain of pressure & anxiety off my shoulders as I plan for a bodacious future!
**John Tyler,**
**Emmy-Award Winning, Multi-Hyphenate Artist**

# A PERSONALIZED GUIDE TO G.R.O.W.
# PRODUCTIVITY
## 100 SELF-PACED STRATEGIES
# just for teens

---

*in memory of Najee and Davon, gone but never forgotten*

---

## acknowledgements

Carissa Harrison

Ajee Hassan

Nikki Ferdinand

Vanessa Lopez

Joseph Davis

Greg & Troy Millings, Rashad Bilal, E. Poe, & Inas Hogans

Yoshi aka Ms. Thomas, Strick, KH, & Gaber

Myeisha & Scott Thompson

Johnson, Ashley & Caelyn Williams, Emily K, Geoff, Proctor, & EB

Sallay K. & Amanda Carter

Josh Austin, Kondwani Fidel, D. Watkins, & Devin Allen

Simon Obas, Ed.D

Baltimore Design School

Woodlands High School

Theodore D. Young Communifty Center of Greenburgh, NY

# HOW TO USE THE FORMULA

**G :**  START WITH PROMPTS TO
**get clear
& confident**

**R :**  APPLY COGNITIVE TOOLS TO
**read &
refocus**

**O :**  ORGANIZE, PLAN, & EXECUTE
**one task
at a time**

**W :**  REFLECT ON YOUR PROGRESS
**when finished,
create**

# CONTENTS

**Fade the habit of procrastinating and amp up your productivity with this workbook featuring 100 strategies for self-determined success!**

**Instead of regular page numbers, we use a special code, like G9, R13, O6, W2, to find each way to grow!**

**It's like a game with 4 rounds:**

**Round 1:  G**

**Round 2:  R**

**Round 3:  O**

**Round 4:  W**

**The aim is to feel really good by engaging in or completing a task all by yourself, using prompts from G to W to help you.**

**Above each prompt, there is a grow-statement to plant positive thoughts in your conscious, before using the strategy.**

# GET CLEAR & CONFIDENT

G1: Describe Yourself

G2: Determination

G3: Goal-Setting

G4: Motivation

G5: Engagement

G6: Intention

G7: Purpose

G8: Abundance

G9: Ease

G10: Stillness

G11: Optimism

G12: Envisioning Celebration

G13: Peace

G14: Boundaries

G15: Read, Watch, Listen

G16: Priorities

G17: After-Journaling Ideas

# READ & REFOCUS

R1: Productive Environment
R2: Reading Plan
R3: Just Start
R4: Start, Space, Start Over
R5: Progress Tally
R6: Study & Stretch
R7: Naming the Noise
R8: Tallying the Noise
R9: Eliminating the Noise
R10: Timelapse
R11: Daydream Monitor
R12: Stamina Graphing
R13: Academic Boredom
R14: Foldables
R15: Vision Board
R16: Personal Reading
R17: Share Your Learning

# ONE TASK AT A TIME

O1: Executive Function Rank
O2: EF Task Checklist
O3: Bitesize Goals
O4: Task Calendar
O5: Organize, Breathe, Start
O6: Hourly Checklist
O7: Task-Specific Checklist
O8: Countdown Timer
O9: Brain-Break
O10: Alternative Starts
O11: Task Perseverance
O12: Self-Check-In
O13: 20/10 Hack
O14: Off-Task Impulses
O15: Self-Compassion List
O16: Timelapse Goal Reminder
O17: Working-Memory

# WHEN FINISHED, CREATE

W1: After-Productivity Ideas
W2: Gratitude Tree
W3: All the Feels Wheel
W4: Dream Catcher
W5: Define Your Success
W6: Personal Progress
W7: Measure Your Success
W8: I Was, I Am
W9: Everything Sheds
W10: I See Myself As
W11: My New Name Means
W12: Framing Reflection
W13: Sensory Reflection
W14: Original Short Story
W15: Patterns and Lines
W16: Dots and Doodles
W17: Creativity Dump

# DIRECTIONS

## 5 WAYS TO USE THIS GUIDE

**1** Use the planning or zine templates on the following pages to customize how you complete G.R.O.W. strategies daily, weekly, or monthly

---

**2** Try:
G prompts before productivity
R + O prompts during productivity
W prompts after productivity

---

**3** Complete the prompts in this book, a digi-notebook, or paper journal

---

**4** Use a board with sticky notes to make a visual, as you track your progress

---

**5** Use the "off-task work space" as a blank journal for thoughts before, during, or after productivity

**Date**

## Creative Goals

### Productivity Checklist

Daily | Weekly | Monthly

### G.R.O.W.Strategies

**G:** _____

**R:** _____

**O:** _____

**W:** _____

### Reflect on 3 Words to Describe Your Growth

_____

_____

_____

**share your growth @g.r.o.w.guide**

# MAKE YOUR OWN ZINE

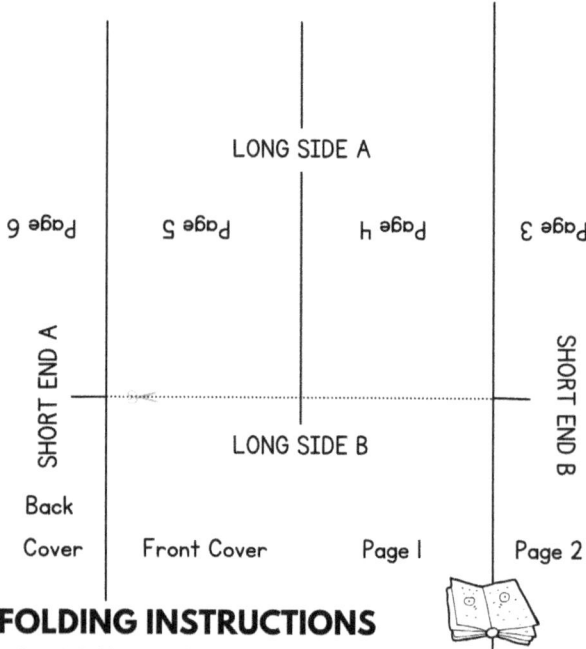

LONG SIDE A

Page 6     Page 5     Page 4     Page 3

SHORT END A

LONG SIDE B

SHORT END B

Back Cover

Front Cover     Page 1     Page 2

## FOLDING INSTRUCTIONS

**Step 1:** Fold on ALL lines. Be sure to make a good crease by using your finger to press the seam firmly.

**Step 2:** Fold in half, placing the Shorts Ends 1 and 2 together and cut on the dotted line segment only.

**Step 3:** Now fold in half the long way, placing Long Sides A and B together, so that you can see a diamond shape where the cut was just made.

**Step 4:** Fold and flatten, pressing the cover to the correct side.

**Step 5:** Create your pages and content according to the instructions. in each segment.

# G.R.O.W. Productivity Guide

Think about
your next step
above

Choose a W
prompt or draw
a self reflection

Choose an O
prompt to
complete below

Compete an
R prompt
above

What's Next?

When Finished,
Create

One Task at a Time

Read & Refocus

New Ideas to GROW

Use the growth
circle below to
capture ideas as
they come
during or after
the session

MY
G.R.O.W.
ZINE

By:

My intention for
this time is to
grow

Get Clear &
Confident

Choose a G
prompt and
complete it
above

Summarize on
the line above

Write your
name above

Write your
intentions above

**USE A BLANK SHEET OF PAPER TO MAKE YOUR OWN ZINE
FOLLOW THE PROMPTS ABOVE OR CREATE YOUR OWN**

# GET CLEAR & CONFIDENT

Graphic organizers
and prompts to guide
you before you start
your productivity
session

**G**

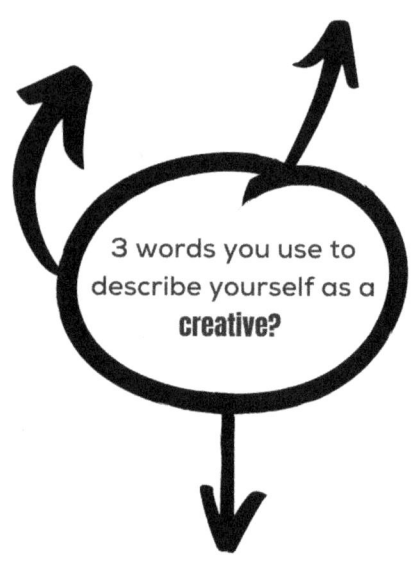

3 words you use to
describe yourself as a
**creative?**

Grow above the noise by staying
focused on your goals

extra thinking space

What are you
**determined**
to complete?

**G2**

Grow beyond limitations to
unleash your full potential

extra thinking space

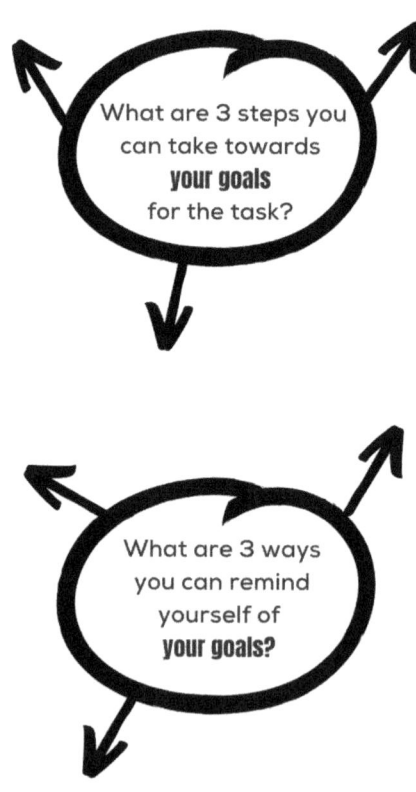

**G3**

Grow through disappointment with
perseverance and determination

extra thinking space

What is the
**motivation**
for your task? Do you
have a personal
connection?

**G4**

Grow above the fear by making
new ways to conquer it

extra thinking space

Grow through failures as stepping stones to success

What can keep you fully **engaged** if you get too distracted from your motivation?

Grow beyond boundaries to explore
new horizons

extra thinking space

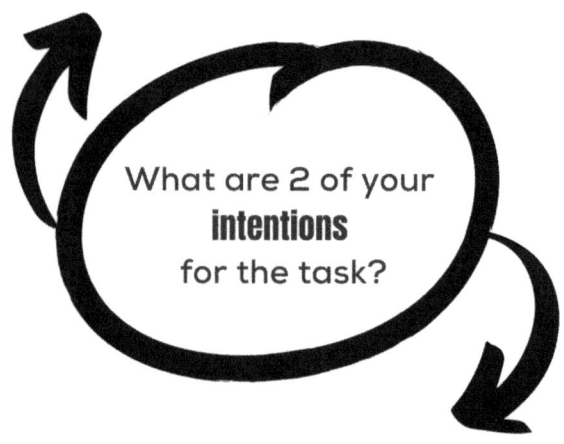

What are 2 of your
**intentions**
for the task?

**G6**

Grow through feedback to
continuously improve and evolve

extra thinking space

What helps to make the
**purpose**
of your task more clear?

Grow through adversity with
resilience and perseverance

Grow beyond trends and spark innovation

extra thinking space

What do you need
to bring you
**ease**
as you produce
creative ideas
or start tasks?

extra thinking space

Grow by striving for excellence in all of
your goals

extra thinking space

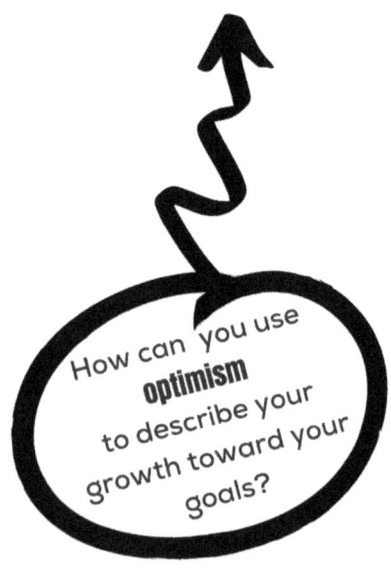

How can you use **optimism** to describe your growth toward your goals?

**G11**

Grow beyond comparison by
focusing on your individual journey

extra thinking space

**G12**

Grow through reflection to gain insights
on your progress and self-awareness

extra thinking space

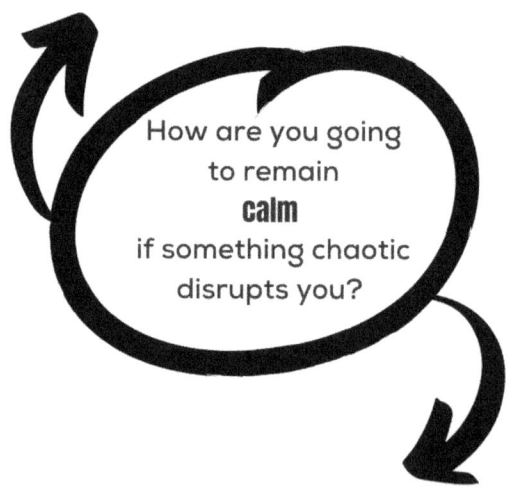

How are you going
to remain
**calm**
if something chaotic
disrupts you?

**G13**

Grow above negativity by
practicing having a positive outlook

extra thinking space

How will you create
**boundaries**
to protect your time,
space, and energy
before starting a
task?

# Grow beyond trends by embracing your unique strengths

extra thinking space

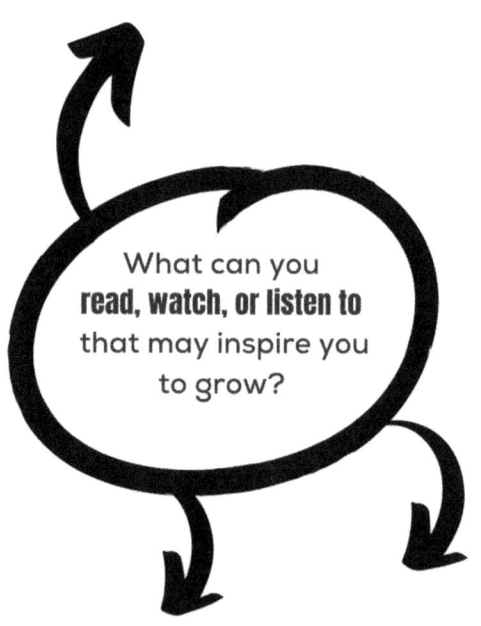

What can you
**read, watch, or listen to**
that may inspire you
to grow?

Grow through uncertainty with
adaptability and flexibility

extra thinking space

How will you
**prioritize**
self-care before you
start your task?

G16

Grow above self-limiting beliefs by
expanding your mindset

extra thinking space

Grow through mistakes as opportunities for learning and growth

## After Journaling Ideas

Set To-Do List
Stretch
Walk
Jog or Run
Full Body Work Out
Bike Ride
Hydrate
Mindful Deep Breaths
Shower
Wash Hands
Eat a Filling Meal
Read
Silent Dancing
Listen to a Podcast or Music
Start a Small Task

**G17**

Grow beyond your past achievements
by setting more challenging goals

extra thinking space

# READ & REFOCUS

During-reading strategies to enhance the focus of your attention on the text

# R

Grow above the distractions with
clarity of goals and vision of success

## Ideas for Setting a Productive Environment

Organize Your Workspace
Set Your Ambiance
Play Calming Music
Set & Track 1 Goal
Visualize Your Success
Drink Lots of Water
Eat Nutritious Snacks
Use a Lumbar Pillow
Put a Plant on Your Desk
Set a Timer
Pre-Plan Guilt-Free Breaks
Remember Your Purpose
Reflect on Your Progress

**R1**

Grow beyond expectations by pushing
the boundaries of what's possible

extra thinking space

## Plan Your Reading Out

Use a calendar to
map out the page
numbers you want to
read in a text. Follow
the calendar as a
way to remind
yourself to meet your
reading goals.

If you miss a day(s)
on your calendar,
move them to
another day. Keep
working with your
own reading schedule
to determine the best
days and times you
are most productive
while reading.

Grow through hard times with
courage and perseverance

extra thinking space

# Just Start

Start a timer and
give yourself 15
minutes to just start.
Try going for 3
rounds to get 45
minutes of
productivity in.
Use the final 15
minutes to take a
break.

If you "just-start"
and have trouble
focusing on
reading,
space out the
reading.

**R3**

Grow above distractions by prioritizing
learning time for personal growth

extra thinking space

## Start, Space, Start Over

If you "just-start" and
have trouble focusing
on reading,
space out the
reading. Do
something else
for 15 minutes,
then start over
with your
reading session.

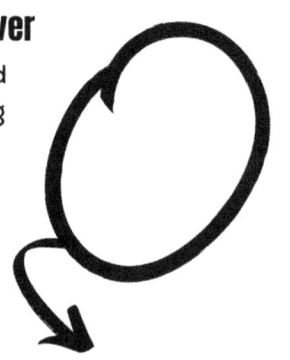

**R4**

Grow beyond unwanted experiences by finding
positive outcomes from what happened

extra thinking space

## Progress Tally

Use a timer to work in 20-30 minute productivity sessions. If you work through the session, without getting distracted, give yourself a tally. After you finish, count how many tally marks you have and create a goal to have more progress tally marks during your next session.

extra thinking space

## Study and Stretch

Set a timer and goal
to be productive for
a 20-30 minute
interval.
After the interval,
take a 10 minute
stretch break. Next,
reset your 20-30
minute timer, create
a new goal, and
complete your
productivity session.

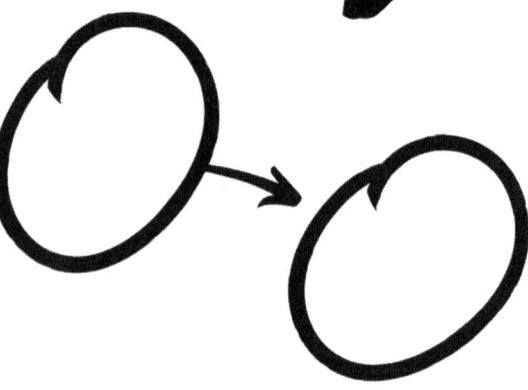

Grow through progress, not just
through success, but also failure

extra thinking space

## Naming the Noise

What are you
hearing in your
mind as you are
trying to focus?
Track your
thoughts with a
focus wheel each
time you notice a
distractive
thought. Title the
wheel once it is
complete.

For example:
"Distracted by My
Friendships" or
"Fears About the
Future" or
"Regrets and
Secrets."

**R7**

Grow through the pages of history through texts
that inform and shape your understanding

extra thinking space

## Tallying the Noise

During productivity,
if you experience a
distracting thought,
use a tally mark
to track the number
of times they occur
but push yourself to
keep focusing  on
completing your
goals beyond the
distractions.

Grow your creativity by trying new ways to express yourself and learning different art techniques

extra thinking space

## Eliminating the Noise

Develop a focus
wheel of 3-4
empowering
thoughts
that may help you
to redirect and
eliminate
mental noises
during productivity
sessions.

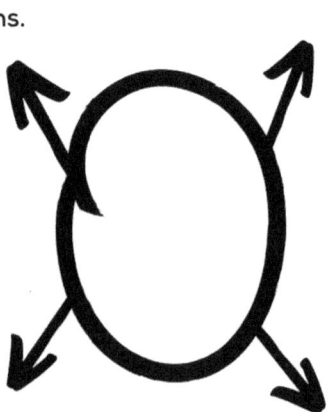

**R9**

Grow beyond trauma by asking experts
for support and healing resources

extra thinking space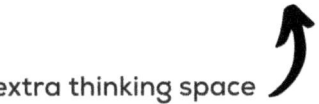

## Timelapse

For self-accountability, use the time-lapse feature of your camera to record yourself during productivity. When you are finished, share your progress using a private or public vlog on YouTube Shorts, TikTok, or Instagram reels.

**R10**

Grow productivity by setting clear
goals and priorities

extra thinking space

## Daydream Monitor

Whether negative or
positive, if you find
yourself daydreaming
while working, take a
break to make a focus
wheel or draw your
visions.
After analyzing
your daydream,
take 10 slow,
deep breaths and
restart your
productivity session.

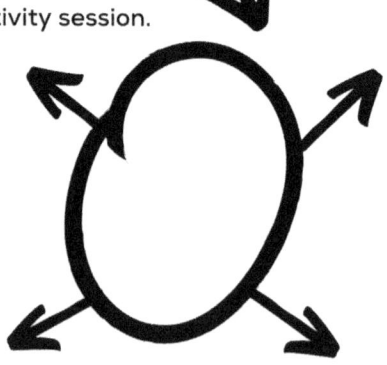

**R11**

Grow beyond trauma by acknowledging
and processing emotions with support

extra thinking space

## Stamina Graphing

Set a goal to build
your current page
number count and/or
minutes of time
reading.

For instance, set a
goal to read 20
pages in 30 minutes.

Create a line, dot, or
bar graph of your
progress. Add to the
graph to show your
progress toward your
goals.

**R12**

Grow understanding of neurodiversity
by listening to diverse point of views

extra thinking space

## Academic Boredom

If you find your
reading assignments
to be so boring that it
is affecting your ability
to understand what
you read, try to make
it more interesting by
listening to the screen
reader (check the
accessibility settings
on your electronic
device) or try finding
video versions of the
readings online.

Use a note catcher  to
capture the gist from
the audio or videos,
then, go back to the
text and test yourself
to see what you
learned and what you
still need to learn.

**R13**

Grow concentration by limiting multitasking
and focusing on one task at a time

extra thinking space

## Foldables

Use index cards or make foldable paper cards for each new idea you learn during productivity.
Use the cards as a reminder of your progress. Recall the information on them, at least 3 times, before moving on. You may want to hang the cards or glue them into a journal in the form of a learning-journey scrapbook. Continue using them to self-test yourself while learning.

Grow productivity by breaking down big
tasks and asking for help when necessary

extra thinking space

## Vision Board

Make a focus wheel to categorize what you envision to be produced as a result of the work you are doing. Create a visual collage of the list by finding photos or words that encompass the list. If digital, make it your screen saver. If you use paper such as sticky notes, hang in your work space. Refer to it when you need motivation to complete your learning task.

**R15**

Grow beyond trauma by finding healthy outlets for self-expression and reflection

extra thinking space

## Personal Reading

Choose a novel, blog post, or comic book that has nothing to do with your tasks. Either read 15 pages or read for 15 minutes.
While reading, escape the world of productivity and focus on the text. After reading, be productive in your work for 20-30 minutes. Start personal reading again, during your next 15 minute break.

**R16**

Grow productivity by learning to prioritize
tasks based on importance and urgency

extra thinking space

## Share Your Learning

If you find yourself
getting distracted by
the excitement or
even the boredom
of your work, develop
a space
to teach others what
you are learning, as
you go.

Try creating a Twitter
or blog/vlog that
allows you to share
keys you highlighted,
study notes, an
outline of main
points,
or a dump of
thoughts you have
about the subject
during your
productivity sessions.

**R17**

Grow productivity by setting boundaries and
saying no to tasks that drain your energy

extra thinking space

# ONE TASK AT A TIME

During-productivity
strategies to enhance
the focus of your
attention on the task

**Number Your Executive Function Strengths & Areas for Growth from 1 to 12**

Initiating a Task

Organizational Routines

Persistence

Impulse Control

Emotional Awareness

TIme Management

Working Memory

Sustained Attention

Planning and Preparation

Flexibility

Social Thinking

Self-Reflection

**O1**

Grow beyond trauma by finding healthy ways to express yourself and process emotions

extra thinking space

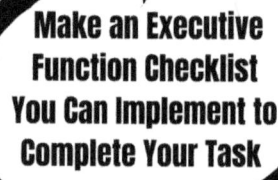

**Make an Executive
Function Checklist
You Can Implement to
Complete Your Task**

- ☐ _____
- ☐ _____
- ☐ _____
- ☐ _____
- ☐ _____
- ☐ _____
- ☐ _____
- ☐ _____
- ☐ _____
- ☐ _____
- ☐ _____
- ☐ _____

Grow by prioritizing self-care and well-being to
fuel your journey of growth

extra thinking space

Break Big Task Goal
into Bitesize Goals

Grow by celebrating progress, no matter how small, and staying focused on the journey ahead

extra thinking space

Determine Your Task Outcome

Break the Task into Smaller Tasks & Use a Digital Calendar with Reminders for the Tasks

Commit to Your Task Calendar

Grow by being grateful and finding
joy in the present moment

extra thinking space

Take 10 Minutes to Organize Your Work Space

Take 10 Minutes to Breathe

Now, Start.

Grow by taking ownership of your choices and actions, and holding yourself accountable

extra thinking space

Grow by improving yourself and your skills through
continuous learning

**Use an Hourly Checklist to Plan Your Day**

- □ 5:00 —————————
- □ 6:00 —————————
- □ 7:00 —————————
- □ 8:00 —————————
- □ 9:00 —————————
- □ 10:00 ————————
- □ 11:00 ————————
- □ 12:00 ————————
- □ 13:00 ————————
- □ 14:00 ————————
- □ 15:00 ————————
- □ 16:00 ————————
- □ 17:00 ————————
- □ 18:00 ————————
- □ 19:00 ————————
- □ 20:00 ————————
- □ 21:00 ————————

**Include your daily distracting tasks
such as texts and social media to
stay engaged and in flow.**

Grow by bouncing back and not giving up

extra thinking space

**Use a Task-Specific Checklist to Pace Yourself**

- ☐ 5:00 ————————————
- ☐ 6:00 ————————————
- ☐ 7:00 ————————————
- ☐ 8:00 ————————————
- ☐ 9:00 ————————————
- ☐ 10:00 ———————————
- ☐ 11:00 ———————————
- ☐ 12:00 ———————————
- ☐ 13:00 ———————————
- ☐ 14:00 ———————————
- ☐ 15:00 ———————————
- ☐ 16:00 ———————————
- ☐ 17:00 ———————————
- ☐ 18:00 ———————————
- ☐ 19:00 ———————————
- ☐ 20:00 ———————————
- ☐ 21:00 ———————————

Grow by focusing on what you love and
doing activities that make you feel excited.

extra thinking space

Grow by staying committed to your goals, even when faced with challenges

Start as Soon as You Sit

Set a 5 Minute Countdown Timer and Just Start

The Goal is to Start within 60 Seconds

Grow by finding inspiration in the success
stories of others to motivate your journey

extra thinking space

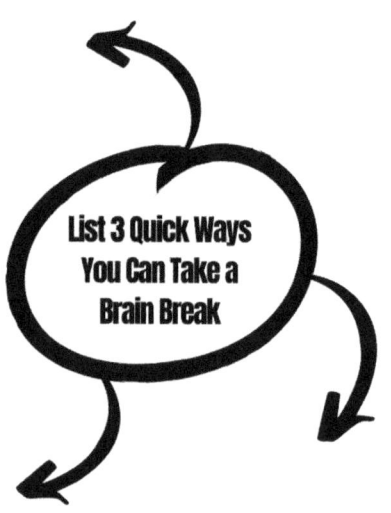

List 3 Quick Ways
You Can Take a
Brain Break

Grow by making sure your actions match your goals

extra thinking space

Give Yourself
Options for
How to Start

Grow by practicing self-reflection
and gaining insight into strengths

extra thinking space

Grow by being proactive and taking initiative to create the outcome you desire

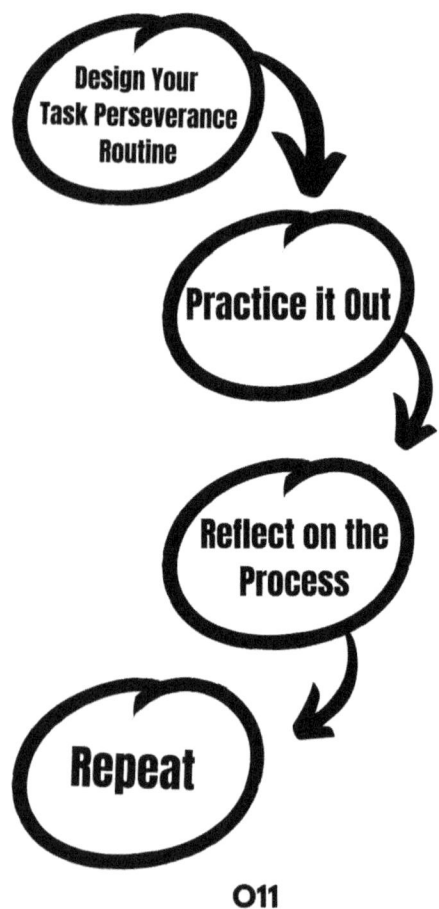

Design Your Task Perseverance Routine

Practice it Out

Reflect on the Process

Repeat

011

Grow by practicing kindness towards yourself
and others, recognizing we are all on a journey

extra thinking space

Grow by challenging yourself to constantly push beyond your limits and expand your potential

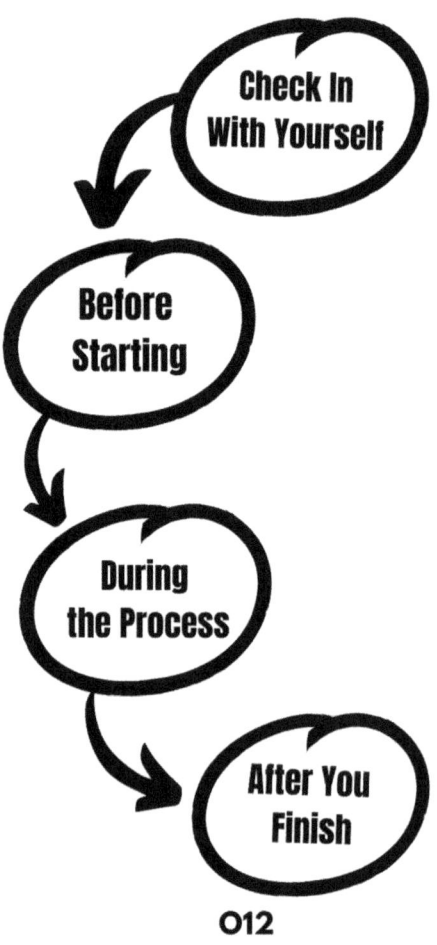

Check In With Yourself

Before Starting

During the Process

After You Finish

012

Grow by embracing progress and pushing
through resistance to reach new heights

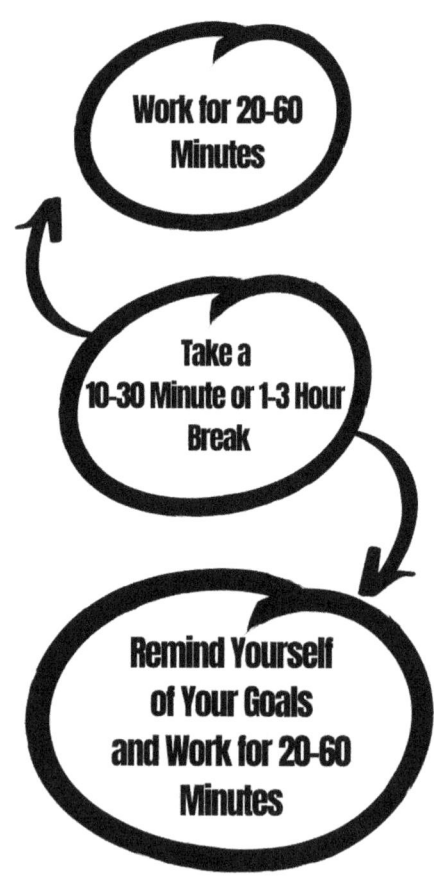

Work for 20-60 Minutes

Take a 10-30 Minute or 1-3 Hour Break

Remind Yourself of Your Goals and Work for 20-60 Minutes

O13

Grow through creative play and exploration

extra thinking space

**Make a List to Self-Monitor Off-Task Impulses**

- [ ] _____
- [ ] _____
- [ ] _____
- [ ] _____
- [ ] _____
- [ ] _____
- [ ] _____
- [ ] _____
- [ ] _____
- [ ] _____
- [ ] _____
- [ ] _____

Grow joy by using creative expression, finding
comfort and strength through the power of art

extra thinking space

Grow the ability to focus by practicing mindfulness
techniques  during creative reflection

**Create a
Self-Compassion List
to Give Yourself
Grace**

- [ ] _____
- [ ] _____
- [ ] _____
- [ ] _____
- [ ] _____
- [ ] _____
- [ ] _____
- [ ] _____
- [ ] _____
- [ ] _____
- [ ] _____
- [ ] _____

**O15**

Grow new ideas by embracing the unknown,
trusting the creative process to lead to discoveries

extra thinking space

Set 2 Goals and Try 2 Rounds of
Using the Timelapse Feature on a
Video Camera to Record Yourself
and Monitor Your Productivity

Grow consistency by establishing daily routines
that support your goals

extra thinking space

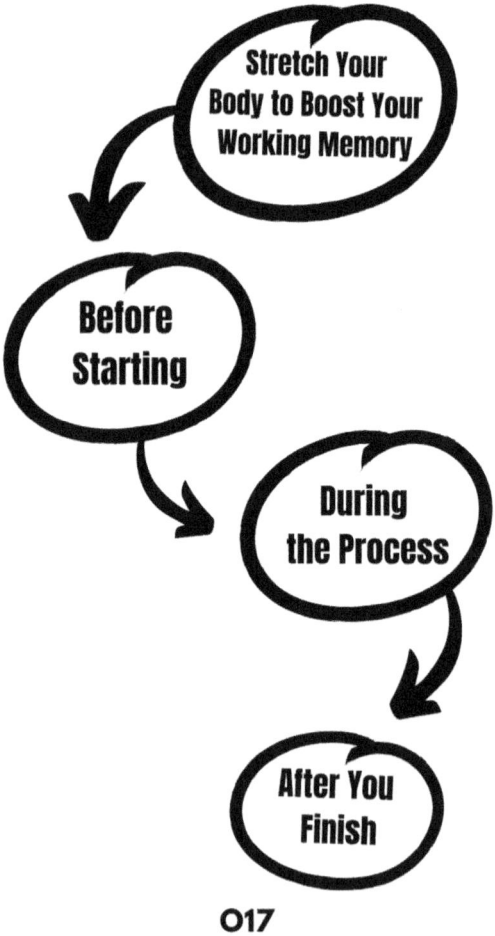

Grow ideas by seeking inspiration
from diverse sources and experiences

Stretch Your
Body to Boost Your
Working Memory

Before
Starting

During
the Process

After You
Finish

Grow consistency by holding yourself
accountable to your responsibilities

extra thinking space

# WHEN FINISHED, CREATE

After-productivity
strategies to
encourage creativity
through reflective
thinking and play

**After-Productivity Ideas**

Rest

Interactive Progress Journal

Mixed-Medium Vlog

Passion Project

Long Walk in Nature

Long Run No Destination

Swim or Ride a Bike

Play a Sport

Nature Watching

Visit a Museum or Garden

Color

Paint

Draw

Binge a TV Show

Bake

**W1**

Grow new ideas by engaging in
brainstorming sessions and creative exercises

extra thinking space

Create a tree of your goals. Add goals as branches of the tree.

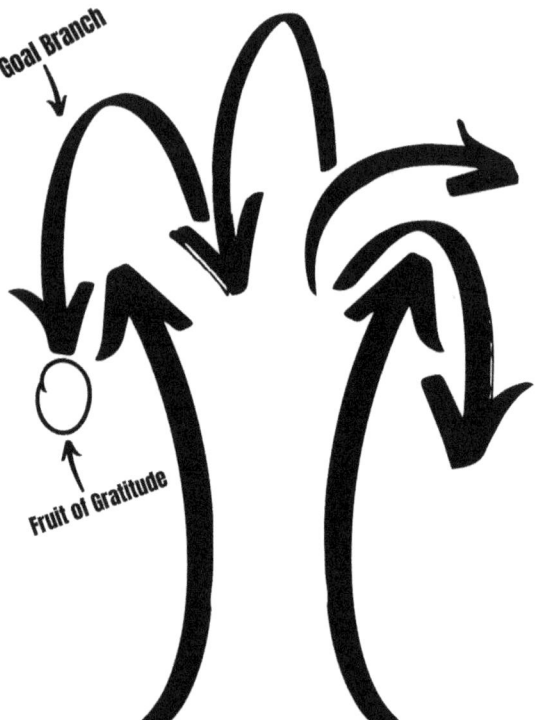

After completion of a goal, add a "fruit of gratitude" to a branch. Use the fruit to write or draw what you are grateful for since completing the goal.

**W2**

Grow ideas by collaborating with others
and embracing different perspectives

extra thinking space

Each time you finish a task, add 1 word
to the focus wheel to describe how you
*feel*:

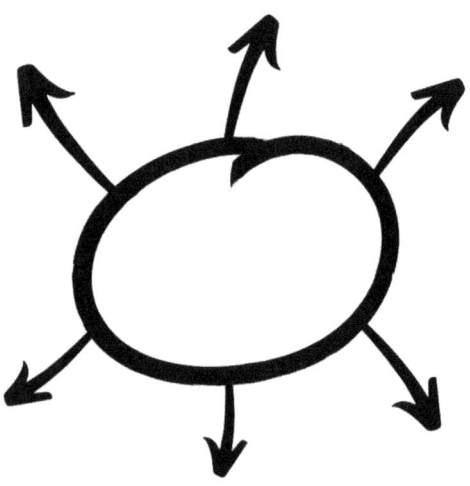

Analyze the trend you find after
completing the focus wheel and add 1
final word in the middle to summarize.
Make art of the words!

**W3**

Grow success by maintaining a positive
mindset and believing in your abilities

extra thinking space

Make your own dream catcher using items to metaphorically represent the dreams you caught by powering through your productivity session.

Start a capsule of your dream catchers by making one each time you finish your task. Hang them all in your work area as a reminder of your goals.

**W4**

Grow consistency by overcoming obstacles
and persevering through challenges

extra thinking space

Each time you finish a task, add 1 word
to the focus wheel to _define_ your
success:

I define my
success as

Analyze the trend you find after filling
the wheel and make art of the words!

**W5**

Grow ideas by seeking feedback from peers and mentors to refine concepts

extra thinking space

List 4 areas you have been able to grow in since you started being more productive

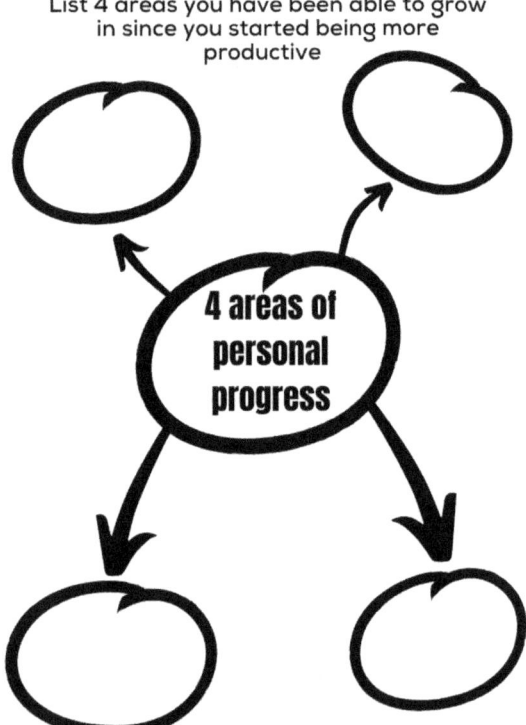

4 areas of personal progress

Create a visual that allows you to map your progress points after you complete a task, in order to see how you are evolving as you learn.

**W6**

Grow ideas by journaling and
capturing thoughts regularly

extra thinking space

How can you *measure* your success
without grades or outside validation?

Create a visual that allows you to
measure your success by your own
standards.

**W7**

Grow success by focusing on the process
rather than solely on the outcome

extra thinking space

Who were you before you started?
Who are you now that you have made
_progress_ toward completing your goals?

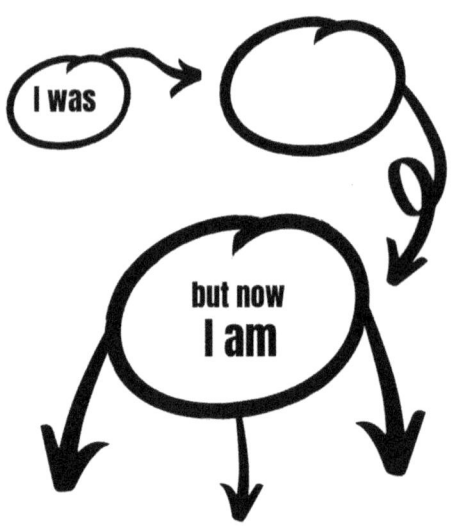

Journal or create self-portraits showing
who you see yourself as.

**W8**

Grow consistency by practicing self-discipline and resisting distractions

Make a list of what you needed to shed and what you still may need to shed as you progress beyond procrastination.

Go for a walk and collect a rock for everything you listed.

Find a body of water or field of dirt to sink or bury all of the rocks you collected, as a symbol of letting go of what no longer serves you.

**W9**

Grow your ideas by exploring how different subjects and topics connect with each other

extra thinking space

First list, then, draw how you see
yourself reaching your goals

As I reach my
goals,
I see myself as

Create a capsule of your drawings to
show your evolution as you completed
your tasks and grew your productivity.

**W10**

Grow consistency by practicing patience
and persistence in pursuit of goals

extra thinking space

Rename yourself when you are in your productive flow. Look up the meaning of this name and create a collage of the words or symbols that help you to visualize the most productive you.

Be sure to develop a healthy balance between the new named you and your sense of true self.

**W11**

Grow ideas by actively seeking out inspiration from a variety of resources

extra thinking space

Choose items from around your house to
make a picture frame.

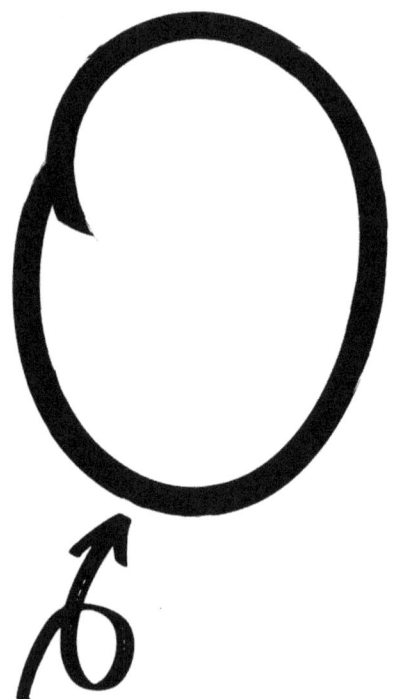

Inside of the frame, add colors, words,
photos, or make a new picture that
allows you to display your growth.

**W12**

Expand your ideas by questioning what you think
you know and the way things are usually done

extra thinking space

What resonates with your senses?

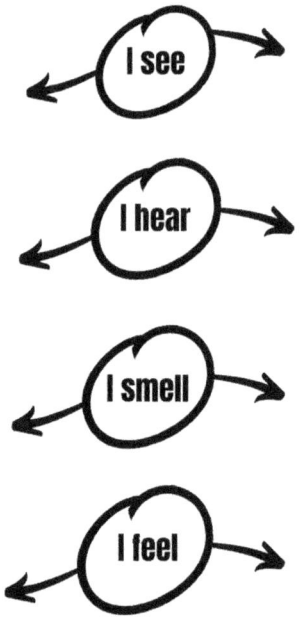

Try this in nature. Use your senses to
create a visual you can hang and
visuallze when you're in your work-flow.

**W13**

Develop new ideas by thinking about things that have happened before and learning from them to help you in the future

extra thinking space

Create a focus wheel of all of the stories in your mind:

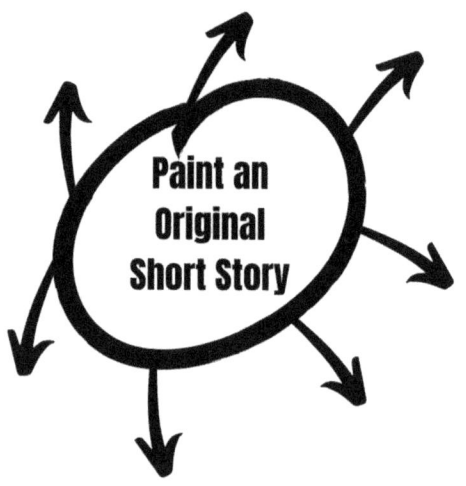

**Paint an Original Short Story**

Choose 1 story to start from the list. Paint it out every time you finish a productivity session.
**W14**

Grow and change by accepting that change can help you grow and become better

Pick up any painting or drawing tools and begin freestylng patterns and dots with colors, shapes, and lines.

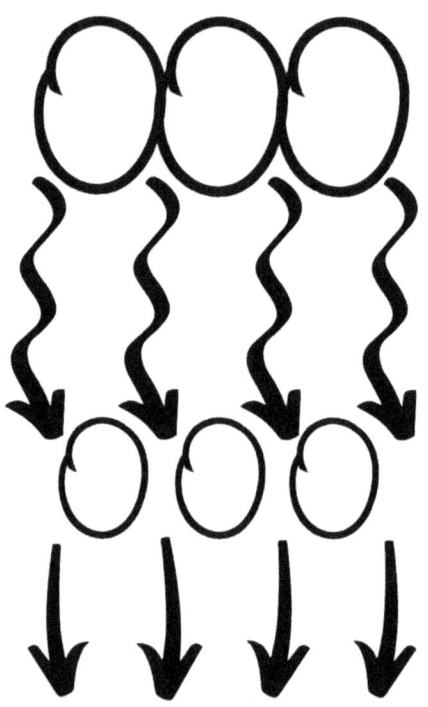

Let your freestyle pattern be a symbol that reflects the different aspect of your progress toward your goals.

**W15**

Grow by challenging limiting beliefs and embracing new possibilities

Create 3-6 layers of doodles by painting or
drawing lines or shapes, after you finish a
task. With each layer, try to fill in blank
spaces.

There is no need to try to make sense of
your doodles. Just enjoy the pleasure of
guilt free play on canvas.

**W16**

Grow success by celebrating progress
and milestones along the journey

extra thinking space

Create a list of all of the small-scale creative projects you ever wanted to try:

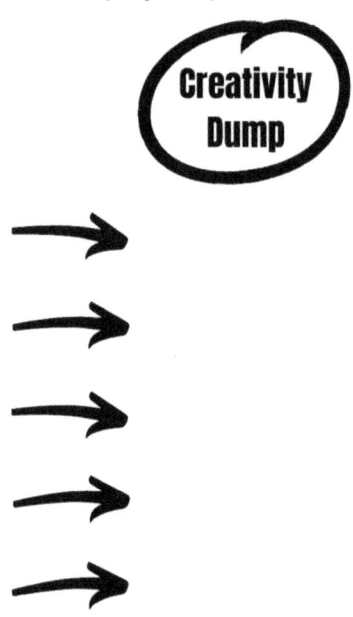

Choose 1 project to start from the list. Work on it every time you finish a productivity session.

**W17**

Grow success by matching what you
do with what you think is important

# How to Use the Blank Pages

**G :** **get clear & confident**
**USE THESE PAGES TO PLAN YOUR DAY AND SET GOALS**

**R :** **read & refocus**
**JOT DOWN YOUR THOUGHTS, NEW LEARNING, AND TRACK READING GOAL PROGRESS**

**O :** **one task at a time**
**ORGANIZE, PLAN, AND KEEP NOTES AS YOU EXECUTE**

**W :** **when finished, create**
**USE THIS SPACE TO ARTFULLY REFLECT AND EXPRESS**

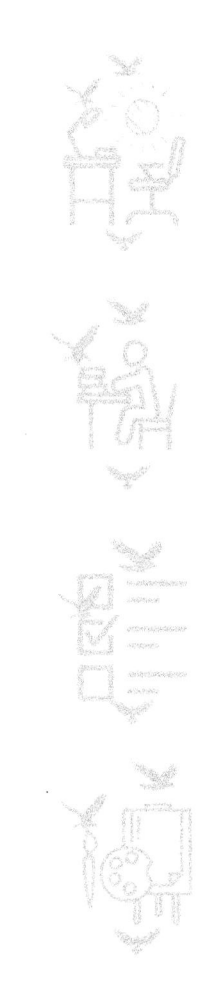

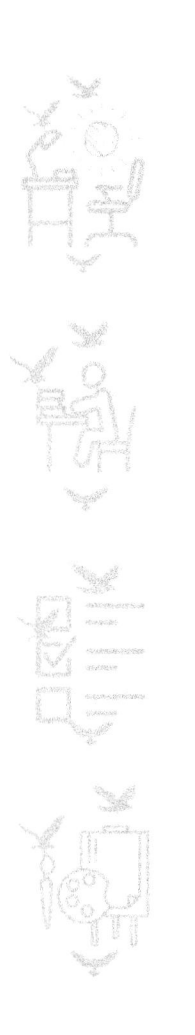

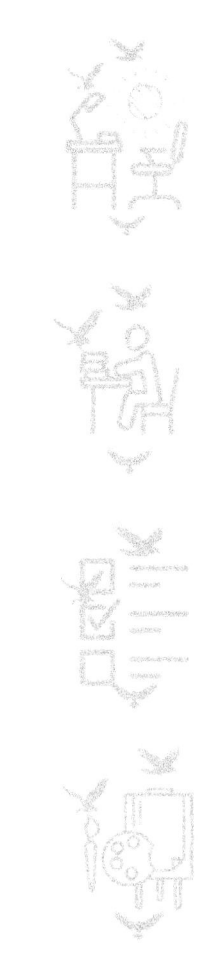

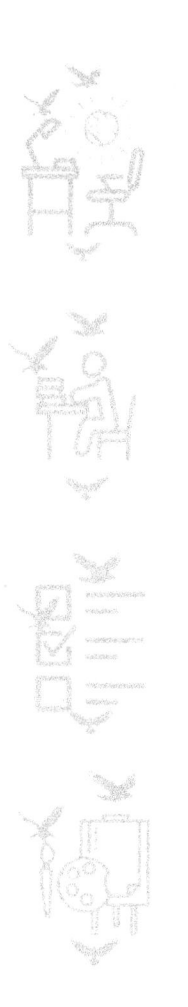

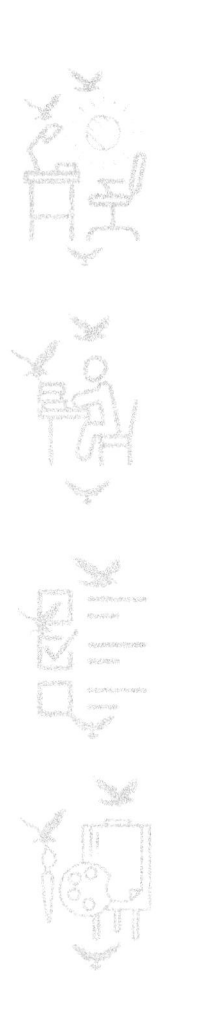

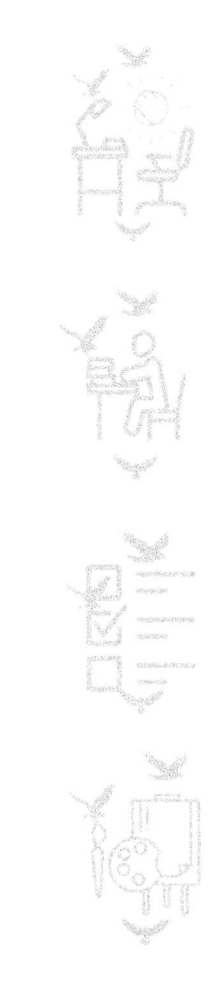

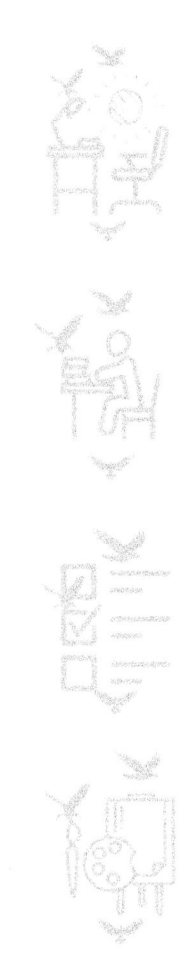

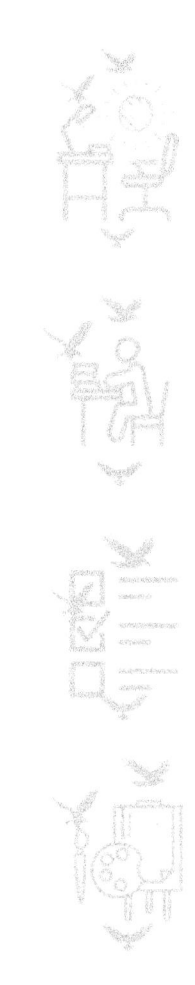

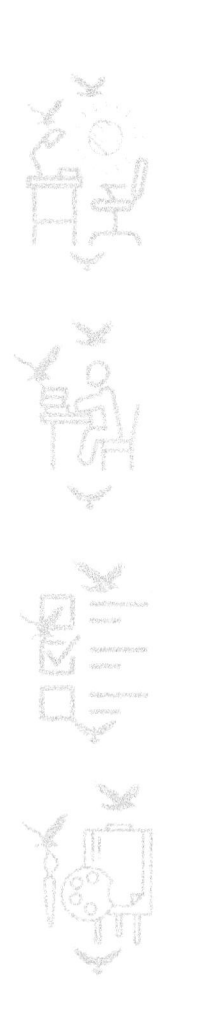

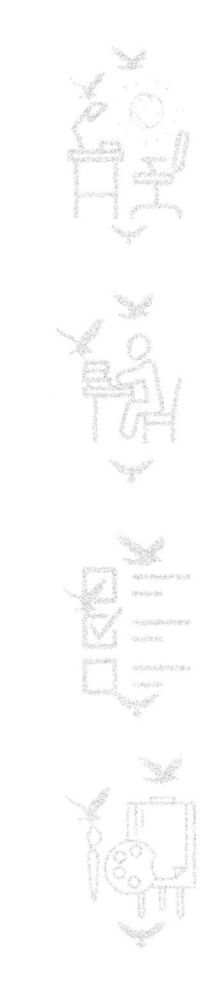

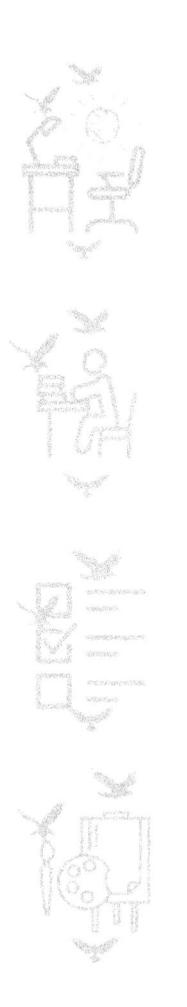

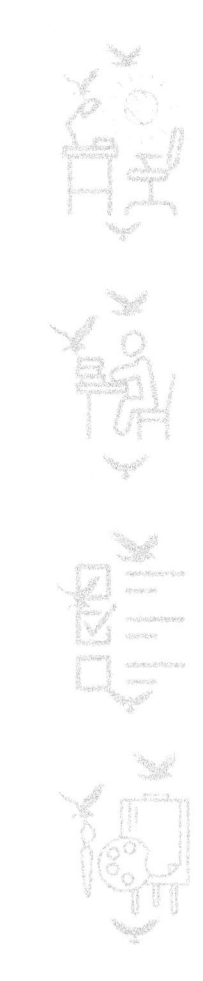

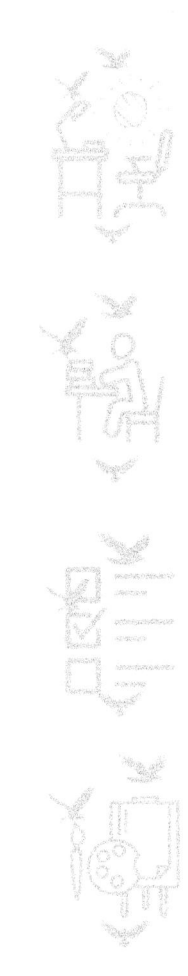

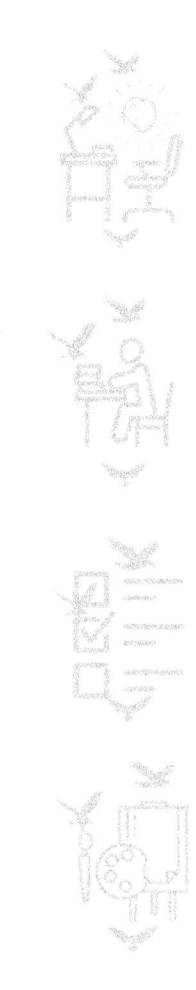

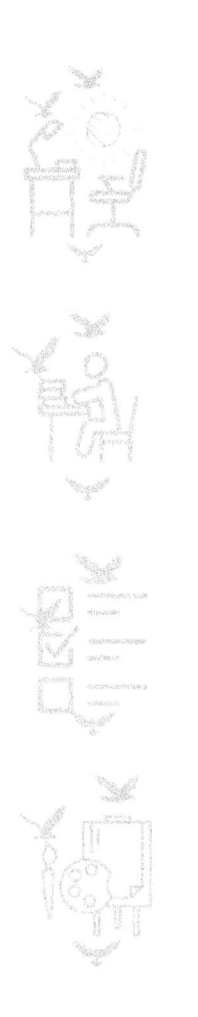

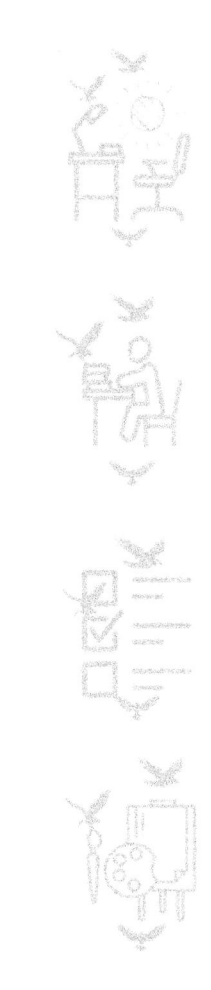

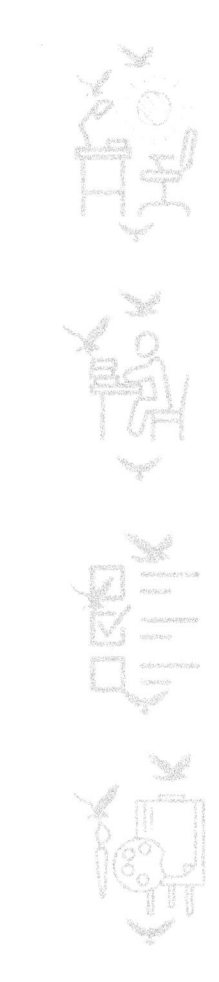

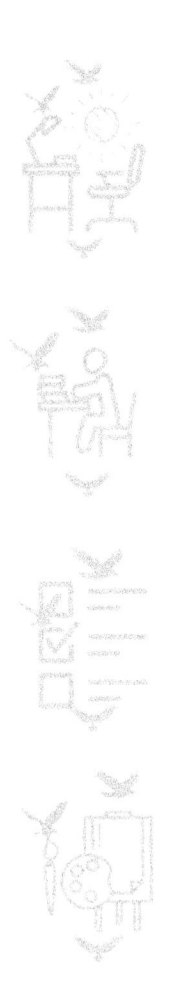

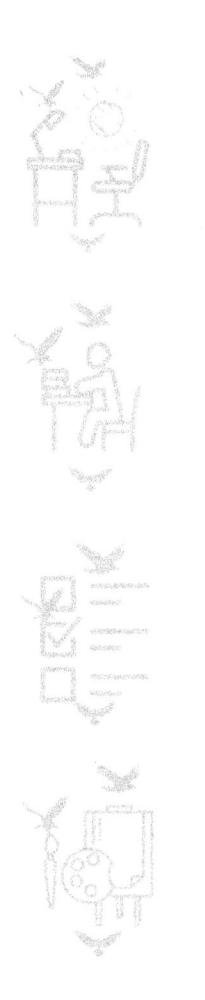

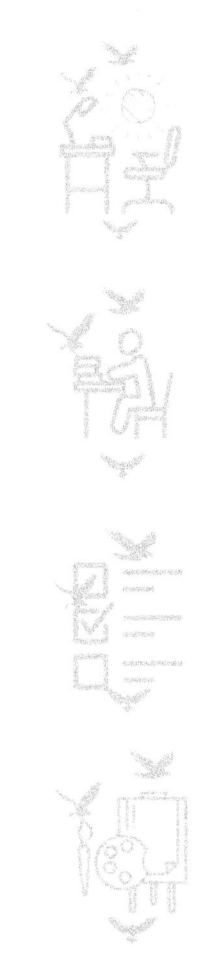

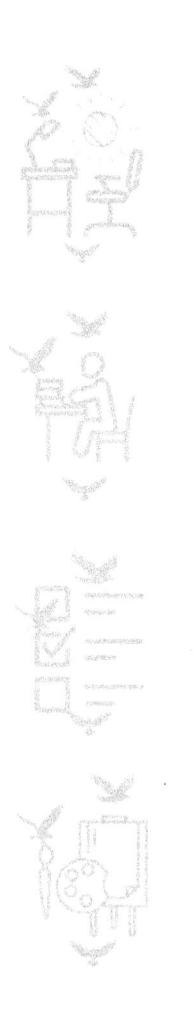

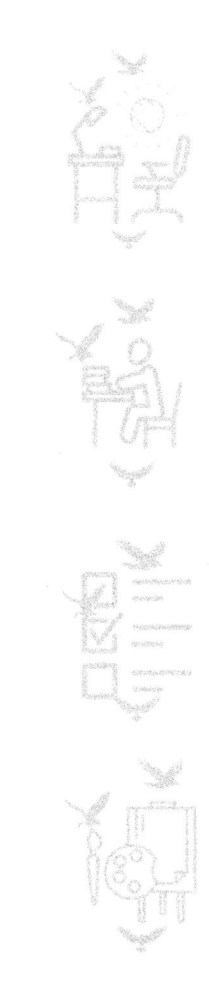

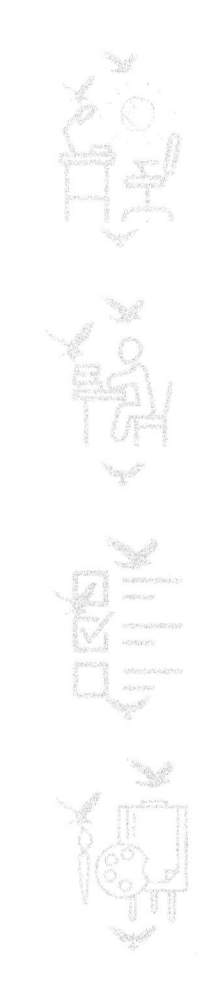

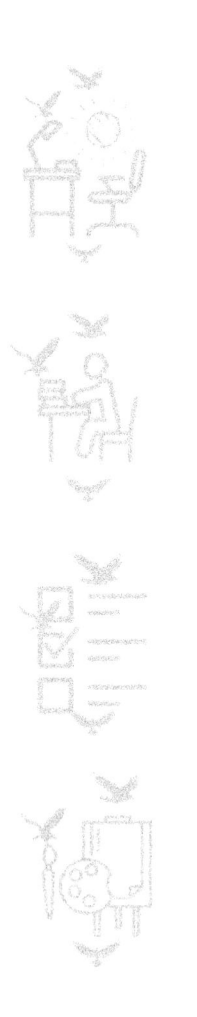

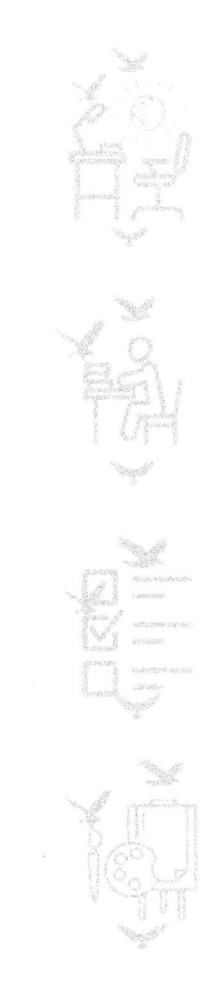

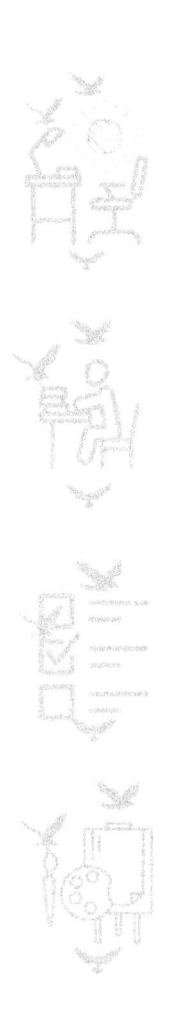

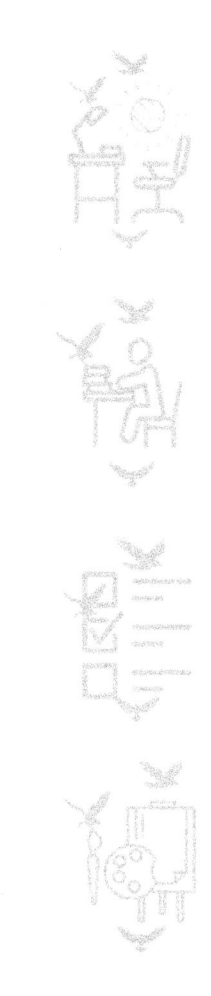

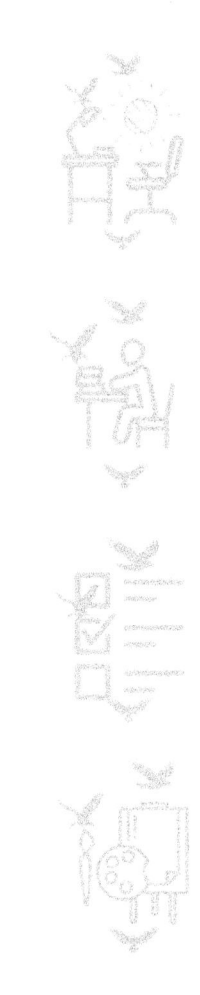

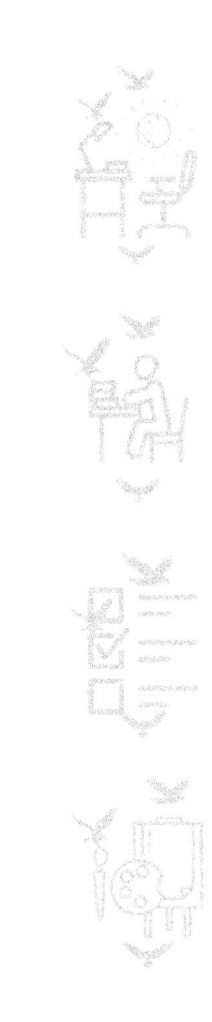

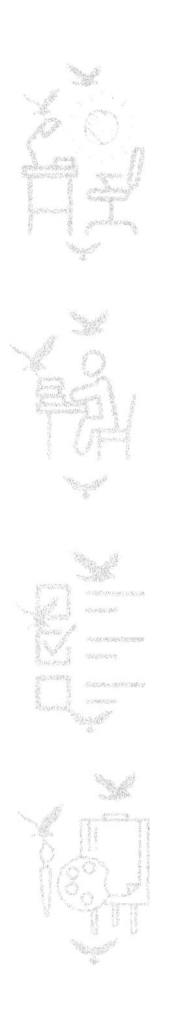

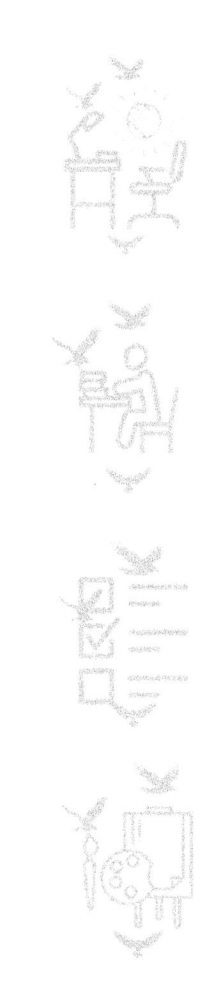

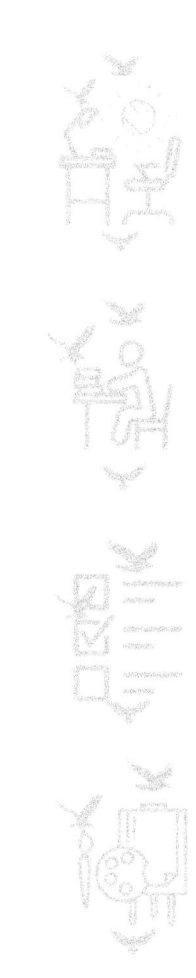

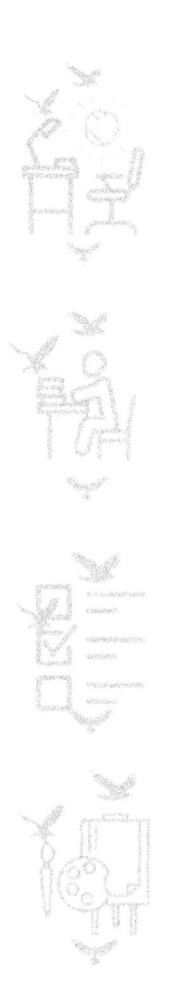

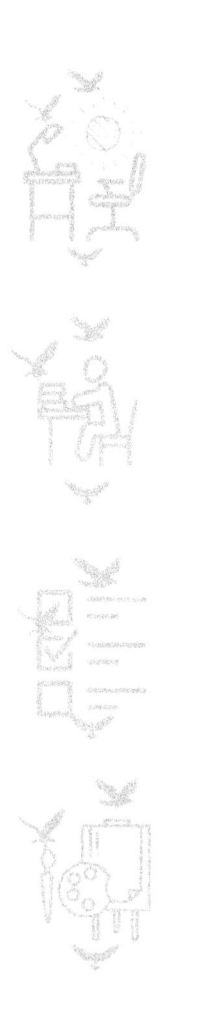

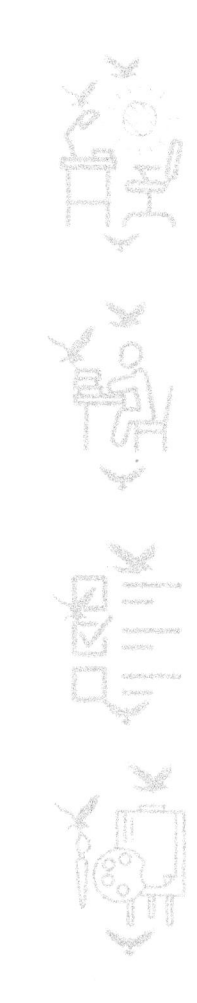

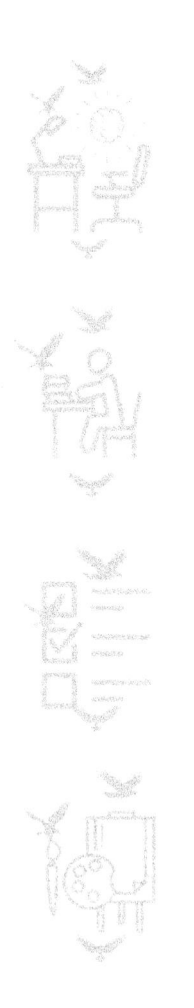

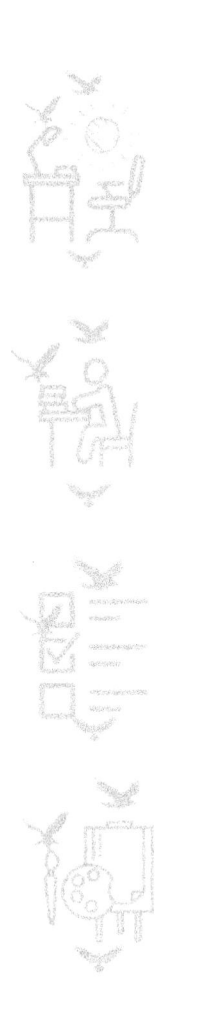

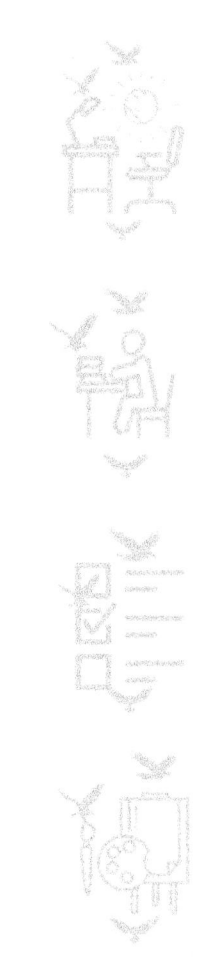

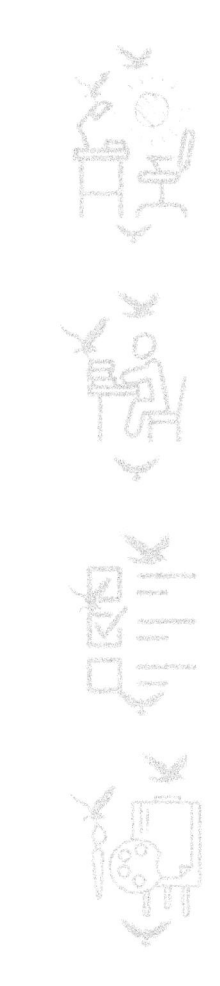

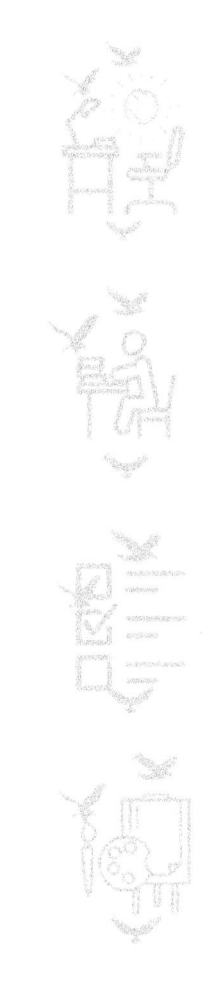

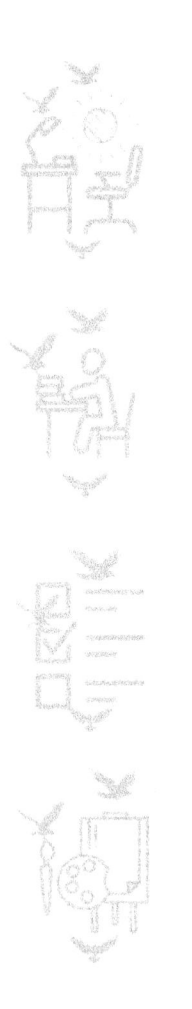

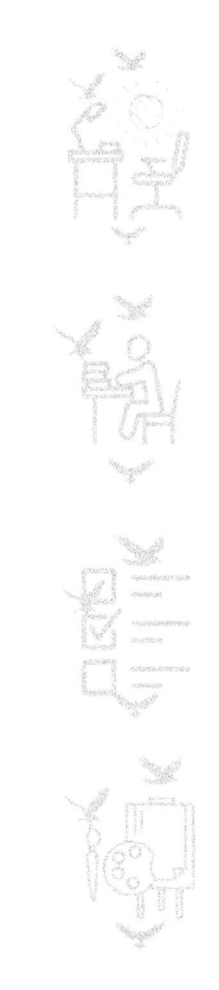

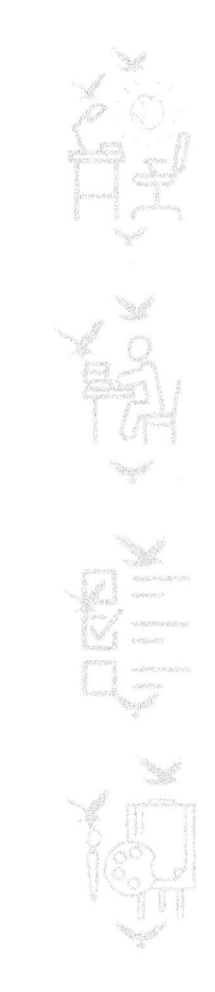

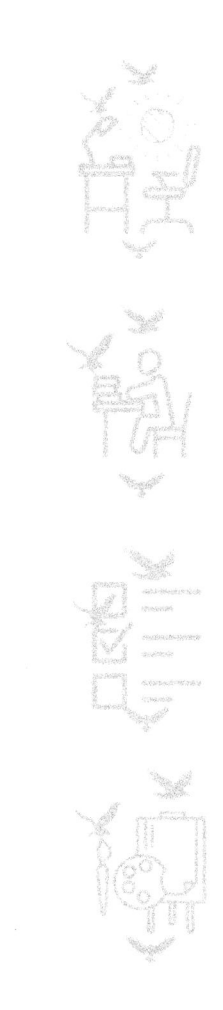

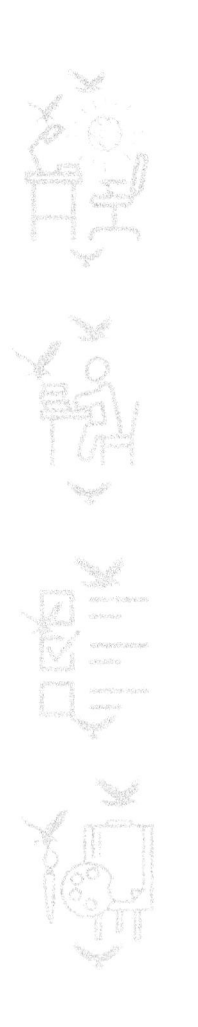

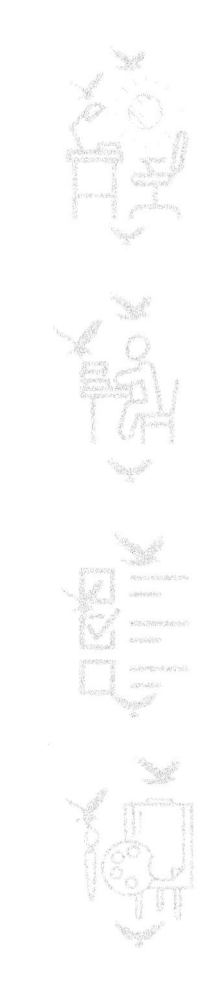

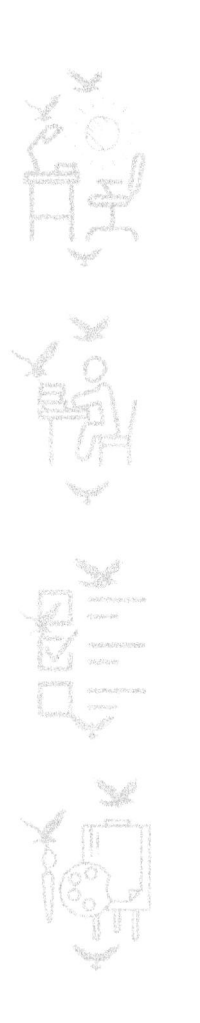

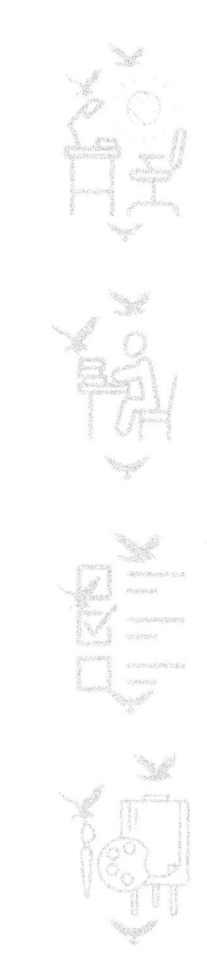

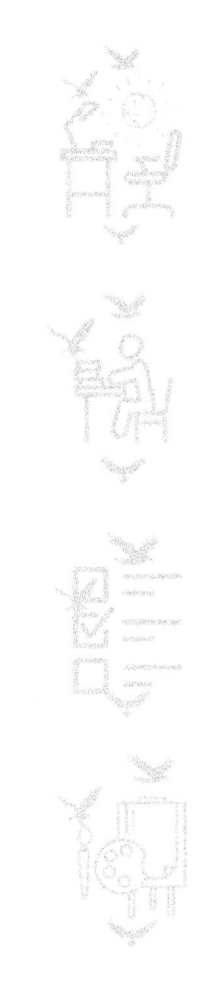

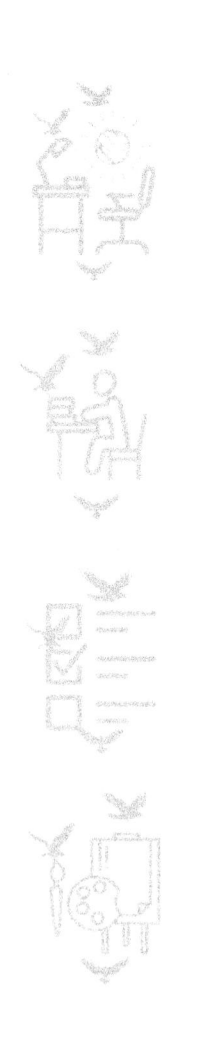

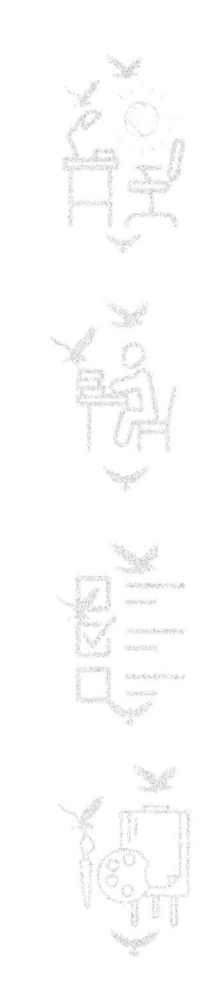

# INDEX

**Canvas**

EXTRA THINKING SPACE    BLANK WORKSPACE
JOURNAL

**Celebration**

G12

**Chaos**

G13

**Checklist**

O2    O6    O7

**Choice**

O10

**Clear**

G3    G4    G6    G7    G10    O5    O12

**Collage**

W11

**Color**

W12    G1

**Doodle**

W16

**Dots**

W16

**Draw**

W10    W15

**Dream Catcher**

W4

**Ease**

G9

**Emotional Awareness**

O12

**Energy**

G14

**Engagement**

G5   R5   R10   R16   O7   08   010   011   013   014   016

**Envisioning**

G12    R15

**Executive Function**

R2    O1–O17

**Flexibility**

O10

**Flow**

O6    O11

**Focus Wheel**

W3

**Foldable**

R14

**Freestyle**

W15    W16

**Goal**

G3    O3

**Grace**
O15

**Graph**

R12

**Graphic Organizer**
G1-16

**Gratitude**
W2

**Growth**
W6

**Guilt-Free**
R1

**Hydrate**
R1

**Impulse Control**
O14

**Nutritious**

G17

**Optimism**

G11

**Organize**

R2   O4   O5

**Outcome**

R15   R17   O3

**Pacing**

O6   O7

**Page Goal**

R2

**Paint**

W15

**Passion Project**

G4   W1

**Priority**

G16

**Procrastination**

W9

**Produce**

G8    G9

**Productive**

R1

**Progress**

R5    O12    W6

**Prompt**

ALL

**Purpose**

G7

**Reading Goal**

R2

**Reels**

R10

**Reflect**

W12

**Reflective Practice**

W12

**Refocus**

R1-17

**Research-Based**

ALL

**Restart**

R4

**Restoration**

W1-17

**Rounds**

O5

**Schedule**

R2   O4   O6   O7

**Scrapbook**

R14

**Self-Accountability**

G3   G16   R5   R10   R11   R12   O4   O6   O7   W6

**Self-Compassion**

G17   O15

**Self-Determination**

G2   R10   O2   O6   O7   W6   W7   W8   W9

**Self-Portrait**

W8

**Share**

R17

**Shed**

W9

**Working-Memory**

O1   O17

**Work Out**

G17   W1

**Workspace**

R11   R14   R15

# References Organized by Tool

**① After Productivity Activities**

Pijpker, R., Kerksieck, P., Tušl, M., De Bloom, J., Brauchli, R., & Bauer, G. F. (2022). The role of off-job crafting in burnout prevention during COVID-19 crisis: a longitudinal study. *International Journal of Environmental Research and Public Health*, 19(4), 2146. https://doi.org/10.3390/ijerph19042146

**② Art as Self-Motivation**

Elbrecht, C. (2019). *Healing trauma with guided drawing: a sensorimotor art therapy approach to bilateral body mapping.* North Atlantic Books.

Isis, P. D., Bush, J., Siegel, C. A., & Ventura, Y. (2010). Empowering students through creativity: art therapy in Miami-Dade county public schools. *Art Therapy*, 27(2), 56–61. https://doi.org/10.1080/07421656.2010.10129712

**③ Before Productivity Activities**

Fiord, N. A. (2003) *Overcoming procrastination: practice the now habit and guilt free play.* MJF Books.

Orbé-Austin, L. & Orbé-Austin, R. (2020) *Own your greatness: overcome impostor syndrome, beat self-doubt, and succeed in life.* Ulysses Press.

Church, M. & Ritchhart, R. (2003) *Making thinking visible: how to promote engagement, understanding, and independence for all learners.* Jossey-Bass.

Ahmed, S. K. (2003) *Being the change: lessons and strategies to teach social comprehension.* Heinemann.

Amen, D. G. (2021) *Your brain is always listening: tame the hidden dragons that control your happiness, habits, and hang-ups.* Tyndale Refresh.

**④ Body Movement**

Bretland, R. J., & Thorsteinsson, E. B. (2015). Reducing workplace burnout: The relative benefits of cardiovascular and resistance exercise. *PeerJ*, 3, e891. https://doi.org/10.7717/peerj.891

Munro, M. (2018). Principles for embodied learning approaches. *South African Theatre Journal.* 31(1), 5–14. https://doi.org/10.1080/10137548.2017.1404435

Rosales-Ricardo, Y., & Ferreira, J. P. (2022). Effects of physical exercise on burnout syndrome in university students. *MEDICC Review*, 24, 36-39. https://doi.org/10.37757/MR2022.V24.N1.7

Wolf, M. R., & Rosenstock, J. B. (2017). Inadequate sleep and exercise associated with burnout and depression among medical students. *Academic Psychiatry*, 41(2), 174-179. https://doi.org/10.1007/s40596-016-0526-y

**⑤ Creating Boundaries**

Fiord, N. A. (2003) *Overcoming procrastination: practice the now habit and guilt free play.* MJF Books.

Glover-Tawwab, N. (2021) *The set boundaries workbook: practical exercises for understanding your needs and setting healthy limits.* TarcherPerigee.

Orbé-Austin, L. & Orbé-Austin, R. (2020) *Own your greatness: overcome impostor syndrome, beat self-doubt, and succeed in life.* Ulysses Press.

### 6 Creative Reflection Questions

Mathisen, G. E., & Bronnick, K. S. (2009). Creative self-efficacy: an intervention study. *International Journal of Educational Research*, 48(1), 21-29.

Maciej Karwowski (Editor), James C. Kaufman (1997). *The creative self: effect of beliefs, self-efficacy, mindset, and identity (explorations in creativity research)* 1st edition. Academic Press.

Beck, H. (2019) *Scatterbrain: how the mind's mistakes make humans creative, innovative, and successful.* Greystone.

### 7 Creativity Theory

Glaveanu, V. P., Hanchett Hanson, M., Baer, J., Barbot, B., Clapp, E. P., Corazza, G. E., ... & Montuori, A. (2019). Advancing creativity theory and research: A socio-cultural manifesto. *The Journal of Creative Behavior*, 1-5. https://doi.org/10.1002/jocb.395

### 8 During Productivity Activities

Hadwin, A. F., Davis, S. K., Bakhtiar, A., & Winne, P. H. (2019). Academic challenges as opportunities to learn to self-regulate learning. *In H. Askell-Williams & J. Orrell (Eds.), Problem Solving for Teaching and Learning.* Routledge https://doi.org/10.4324/9780429400902-4

Miyatsu, T., Nguyen, K., & McDaniel, M. A. (2018). Five popular study strategies: Their pitfalls and optimal implementations. *Perspectives on Psychological Science*, 13(3), 390–407. https://doi.org/10.1177/1745691617710510

Muijs, D., & Bokhove, C. (2020). *Metacognition and self-regulation: evidence review.* Education Endowment Foundation.

Pérez-Álvarez, R., Maldonado-Mahauad, J., & Pérez-Sanagustín, M. (2018). Tools to support self-regulated learning in online environments: literature review. *In European Conference on Technology Enhanced Learning.* Springer, Cham.

Serravallo, J. (2015). *The reading strategies book: your everything guide to developing skilled readers.* Portsmouth, NH: Heinemann.

van de Pol, J., van Loon, M., van Gog, T., Braumann, S., & de Bruin, A. (2020). Mapping and drawing to improve students' and teachers' monitoring and regulation of students' learning from text: current findings and future directions. *Educ Psychol Rev 32*, 951–977 (2020). https://doi.org/10.1007/s10648-020-09560-y

### 9 Elaboration & Transfer

Brown, P.C. (2014). *Make it stick: the science of successful learning.* Harvard University Press.

Eraut, M. (2009). 2.1 Transfer of knowledge between education and workplace settings. In H. Daniels, H. Lauder, & J. Porter (Eds.), *Knowledge, values and educational policy: a critical perspective* (pp. 53–73). Routledge.

### 10 Engagement

Csikszentmihalyi, M. (2008). Flow: The Psychology of Optimal Experience World. Grand Central Publishing.

Newport, C. (2017). Deep Work: Rules for Focused Success in a Distracted World. Grand Central Publishing.

Stobaugh, R. (2019). *Fifty strategies to boost cognitive engagement: creating a thinking culture in the classroom - 50 teaching strategies to support cognitive development.* Solution Tree Press.

### 11 Emotions

Arguedas, M., Daradoumis, T., & Xhafa, F. (2016). *Analyzing how emotion awareness influences students' motivation, engagement, self-regulation and learning outcome. Educational Technology & Society*, 19(2), 87–103. http://www.jstor.org/stable/jeductechsoci.19.2.87

Trenton, N. (2021) *Stop overthinking: 23 techniques to relieve stress, stop negative spirals, declutter your mind, and focus on the present.* NCTS, Inc.

# G.R.O.W. Productivity Guide

**(12)** **Executive Function**

Executive function strategies blog posts. ThePathway2Success.com. Retrieved September 2022

Johnson, J., & Reid, R. (2011). Overcoming executive function deficits with students with ADHD. *Theory into Practice*, 50(1), 61–67. https://doi.org/10.1080/00405841.2010.534942

Mitsea, E. & Drigas, A. (2019). A journey into the metacognitive learning strategies. *International Journal of Online and Biomedical Engineering (iJOE)*, 15(14), pp. 4–20. https://doi.org/10.3991/ijoe.v15i14.11379

Otero, T. M., Barker, L. A., & Naglieri, J. A. (2014). Executive function treatment and intervention in schools. *Applied Neuropsychology: Child*, 3(3), 205–214. https://doi.org/10.1080/21622965.2014.897903

**(13)** **Future-Time Perspective**

Bembenutty, H., & Karabenick, S. A. (2004). Inherent association between academic delay of gratification, future time perspective, and self-regulated learning. *Educational Psychology Review* 16, 35–57. https://doi.org/10.1023/B:EDPR.0000012344.34008.5c

Rosenzweig, E. Q., Hulleman, C. S., Barron, K. E., Kosovich, J. J., Priniski, S. J., & Wigfield, A. (2019). Promises and pitfalls of adapting utility value interventions for online math courses. *Grantee Submission*, 87(2), 332–352 https://doi.org/10.1080/00220973.2018.1496059

Schuitema, J., Peetsma, T., & van der Veen, I. (2014). Enhancing student motivation: a longitudinal intervention study based on future time perspective theory. *Journal of Educational Research*, 107(6), 467–481. http://dx.doi.org/10.1080/00220671.2013.836467

Tsai, M.-Y. (2015). The Relationships among Imagination, Future Imagination Tendency, and Future Time Perspective of Junior High School Students. *Universal Journal of Educational Research*, 3(3), 229–236. https://doi.org/10.13189/ujer.2015.030309

**(14)** **Goal-Setting**

Boot, N., Nevicka, B., & Baas, M. (2020). Creativity in ADHD: goal-directed motivation and domain specificity. *Journal of Attention Disorders*, 24(13), 1857–1866. https://doi.org/10.1177/1087054717727352

Muis, K. R., Ranellucci, J., Franco, G. M., & Crippen, K. J. (2013). The interactive effects of personal achievement goals and performance feedback in an undergraduate science class. *Journal of Experimental Education*, 81(4), 556–578. https://doi.org/10.1080/00220973.2012.738257

Wehmeyer, M., Hughes, C., Agran, M., Garner, N., & Yeager, D. (2003). Student-directed learning strategies to promote the progress of students with intellectual disability in inclusive classrooms. *Int. J. Inclusive Education*, 7(4), 415-428. https://doi.org/10.1080/1360311032000110963

**(15)** **Gratitude**

Bono, G., & Sender, J. T. (2018). How gratitude connects humans to the best in themselves and in others. *Research in Human Development*, 15(3-4), 224-237. https://doi.org/10.1080/15427609.2018.1499350

**(16)** **Internal Distractions**

Schleider, J. L., Mullarkey, M. C., & Dobias, M. L. (2021) *The growth mindset workbook for teens: say yes to challenges, deal with difficult emotions, and reach your full potential.* Instant Help.

Helmstetter, S. (2014) *The Power of neuroplasticity.* Park Avenue Press.

Responsive Classroom (2016) *Responsive classroom refocus and recharge! 50 brain breaks for middle schoolers.* Center for Responsive Schools, Inc.

**(17)** **Mind Mapping**

Knight, K. (2012) *Mind mapping: improve memory, concentration, communication, organization, creativity, and time management.* Mind Lil

## 18 Motivation

Nagashibaevna, Y. K. (2019). Students' lack of interest: how to motivate them? *Universal Journal of Educational Research*, 7(3), 797–802. https://doi.org/10.1111/1467-9604.12340

Mendler, A. N. (2021) *Motivating students who don't care: proven strategies to engage all learners, second edition*. Solution Tree Press

## 19 Outdoors Activities

Barnes, M. R., Donahue, M. L., Keeler, B. L., Shorb, C. M., Mohtadi, T. Z., & Shelby, L. J. (2019). Characterizing nature and participant experience in studies of nature exposure for positive mental health: An integrative review. *Frontiers in Psychology*, 9, 2617. https://doi.org/10.3389/fpsyg.2018.02617

Meredith, G. R., Rakow, D. A., Eldermire, E. R., Madsen, C. G., Shelley, S. P., & Sachs, N. A. (2020). Minimum time dose in nature to positively impact the mental health of college-aged students, and how to measure it: A scoping review. *Frontiers in Psychology*, 2942. https://doi.org/10.3389/fpsyg.2019.02942

## 20 Procrastination

Fiord, N. A. (2003) *Overcoming procrastination: practice the now habit and guilt free play*. MJF Books.

Fishbach, A. (2022) *Get it done: surprising lessons from the science of motivation*. Little Brown Spark

Lieberman, C. (2019). *Why you procrastinate (it has nothing to do with self-control)*. New York Times, 25.

## 21 Productive Environment

Lisa, S. N., & Dwiyanti, E. (2022). Literature study of work accompaniment music to effect on employee productivity in several companies. *Journal of Public Health Research and Community Health Development*, 5(2), 73-79. http://dx.doi.org/10.20473/jphrecode.v5i2.26528

McLoughlin, C., & Lee, M. J. W. (2010). Personalised and Self Regulated Learning in the Web 2.0 Era: International Exemplars of Innovative Pedagogy Using Social Software. *Australasian Journal of Educational Technology*, 26(1), 28–43. https://doi.org/10.14742/ajet.1100

## 22 Progress Tracker

Ayobi, A., Sonne, T., Marshall, P., & Cox, A. L. (2018). Flexible and mindful self-tracking: design implications from paper bullet journals. In *Proceedings of the 2018 CHI Conference on Human Factors in Computing Systems* (pp. 1-14). https://doi.org/10.1145/3173574.3173602

Fiord, N. A. (2003) *Overcoming procrastination: practice the now habit and guilt free play*. MJF Books.

Fishbach, A. (2022) *Get it done: surprising lessons from the science of motivation*. Little Brown Spark

Marwan, S., Shabrina, P., Milliken, A., Menezes, I., Catete, V., Price, T. W., & Barnes, T. (2021). Promoting students' progress-monitoring behavior during block-based programming. In *21st Koli Calling International Conference on Computing Education Research* (pp. 1-10). https://doi.org/10.1145/3488042.3488064

## 23 Reflective Practice

Carroll, R. (2018). *The bullet journal method: track the past, order the present, design the future*. New York, New York: Portfolio/Penguin.

Mezirow, J. (1998). On critical reflection. *Adult Education Quarterly*, 48(3), 185-198.

Rogers, S. (1997) *Motivation & learning: a teacher's guide to building excitement for learning & igniting the drive for quality*. Peak Learning Systems

**24** **Rest**

Wolf, M. R., & Rosenstock, J. B. (2017). Inadequate sleep and exercise associated with burnout and depression among medical students. *Academic Psychiatry*, 41(2), 174-179 https://doi.org/10.1007/s40596-016-0526-y

**25** **Self-Actualization**

Hill, C. L., & Updegraff, J. A. (2012). Mindfulness and its relationship to emotional regulation. *Emotion*, 12(1), 81–90. https://doi.org/10.1037/a0026355

Lanaj, K., Foulk, T. A., & Erez, A. (2019). Energizing leaders via self-reflection: A within-person field experiment. *Journal of Applied Psychology*, 104(1), 1. https://doi.org/10.1037/apl0000350

**26** **Self-Determination**

Ryan, R. M. & Deci, E. L. (2018) *Self-determination theory: basic psychological needs in motivation, development, and wellness.* The Guilford Press.

**27** **Self-Regulatory Learning**

Bjork, R. A., Dunlosky, J., & Kornell, N. (2013). Self-regulated learning: beliefs, techniques, and illusions. *Annual Review of Psychology*, 64(1), 417–444. https://doi.org/10.1146/annurev-psych-113011-143823

Cho, M.-H., & Heron, M. L. (2015). Self-regulated learning: the role of motivation, emotion, and use of learning strategies in students' learning experiences in a self-paced online mathematics course. *Distance Education*, 36(1), 80–99. https://doi.org/10.1080/01587919.2015.1019963

Cleary, T. J., & Platten, P. (2013). Examining the correspondence between self-regulated learning and academic achievement: a case study analysis. *Education Research International*, https://doi.org/10.1155/2013/272560

Reddy, L. A., Cleary, T. J., Alperin, A., & Verdesco, A. (2018). A critical review of self-regulated learning interventions for children with attention-deficit hyperactivity disorder. *Psychology in the Schools*, 55(6), 609–628. https://doi.org/10.1002/pits.22142

Wehmeyer, M., Hughes, C., Agran, M., Garner, N., & Yeager, D. (2003). Student-directed learning strategies to promote the progress of students with intellectual disability in inclusive classrooms. *Int. J. Inclusive Education*, 7(4), 415-428. https://doi.org/10.1080/1360311032000110963

**28** **Storytelling as Therapy**

Ricks, L., Kitchens, S., Goodrich, T., & Hancock, E. (2014). My story: The use of narrative therapy in individual and group counseling. *Journal of Creativity in Mental Health*, 9(1), 99-110. https://doi.org/10.1080/15401383.2013.870947

**29** **Summarizing & Generation**

Brown, P.C. (2014). *Make it stick: the science of successful learning.* Harvard University Press.

Hao, N., Ku, Y., Liu, M., Hu, Y., Bodner, M., Grabner, R. H., & Fink, A. (2016). Reflection enhances creativity: Beneficial effects of idea evaluation on idea generation. *Brain and Cognition*, 103, 30–37. https://doi.org/10.1016/j.bandc.2016.01.005

Roediger, H. L., III, & Butler, A. C. (2010). The critical role of retrieval practice in long-term retention. *Trends in Cognitive Science*, 15(1), 20–27. https://doi.org/10.1016/j.tics.2010.09.003

**30** **Visualization**

Waalkes, P. L., Gonzalez, L. M., & Brunson, C. N. (2019). Vision boards and adolescent career counseling: A culturally responsive approach. *Journal of Creativity in Mental Health*, 14(2), 205-216.

# GROW WITH US

Hey there, Creative!

Think of this guide as your personal productivity pad! It's from Growcery Garden, a bookshop where all sorts of creative minds come together. Whether you're an artist, a leader, a writer, or anything in between, we're here to help.

At Growcery Garden, we've got tools to help you boost your productivity:

- Strategies for learning on your own
- Playlists to keep you inspired
- Virtual workshops
- Live productivity parties

Oh, and here's a little reminder: Before you explore our website or use our resources, talk to your guardians or teachers, first. They can help you make the most out of the G.R.O.W. formula and the resources we offer.

Ready to see your creativity come to life? Head over to growcerygarden.org and let's grow together!

**Valenciá and Fabian D. Bell**
**Author/Designer and Publisher/Producer**

*Growcery Garden*

BOOKSHOP & CREATIVE COMMUNITY
ROOTED IN PRODUCTIVITY & PROSPERITY